ENVIRONMENTAL
DISASTERS

John Baines

Thomson Learning
New York

BOOKS IN THIS SERIES

AIR DISASTERS

ENVIRONMENTAL DISASTERS

NATURAL DISASTERS

SEA DISASTERS

Cover
(Background) This forest has been destroyed by acid rain.
Air pollution, such as smoke and chemicals, mixes with
clouds and then falls as acid rain, which poisons trees,
plants, rivers, and lakes.
(Inset) The Kuwaiti oil-well fires were a terrible
environmental disaster for the people, animals, and plant
life in the Persian Gulf region.

First published in the United States in 1993 by
Thomson Learning
115 Fifth Avenue
New York, NY 10003

First published in 1993 by Wayland (Publishers) Ltd.

Copyright © 1993 Wayland (Publishers) Ltd.

U.S. version copyright © 1993 Thomson Learning

Library of Congress Cataloging-in-Publication Data
Baines, John D.
  Environmental disasters / John Baines. – U.S. revision
        p.   cm. – (The World's disasters)
  Includes bibliographical references (p.   ) and index.
  Summary: A history of environmental disasters, including both
natural and man-made.
  ISBN 1-56847-086-X : $15.95
  1. Environmental degradation – Juvenile literature. 2. Natural
disasters – Juvenile literature. [1. Natural disasters. 2. Environmental
protection.] I. Title. II. Series.
GE140.5.B37   1993
363.73 – dc20   93-8526

Printed in Italy

CONTENTS

WE NEED A CLEAN ENVIRONMENT   4

NUCLEAR DANGER   7

CHEMICAL HAZARDS   14

POISONED WATERS   19

WASTE NOT, WANT NOT   23

OIL ON THE WATERS   28

AT WAR WITH THE ENVIRONMENT   32

STRIPPING THE EARTH   38

DANGER IN THE AIR   43

GLOSSARY   46

FURTHER READING   47

INDEX   48

WE NEED A CLEAN ENVIRONMENT

The environment is everything that surrounds us. Our environment includes natural surroundings as well as things that are made by people, such as buildings, roads, furniture, and machines.

People, like all living things, need a clean and healthy environment to survive. The natural environment provides us with the water, food, and air we need to stay alive and the land on which to live. It also provides raw materials, which are used to build houses or make clothes, household goods, books, television sets, and many other items that make our lives more comfortable. In turn, the actions of humans affect the environment. Every time we cut down a forest or dump waste products into rivers, we change the environment.

It is important to take care of the environment so that it can continue to support all living things.

WHAT ARE ENVIRONMENTAL DISASTERS?

There are many types of environmental disasters. Some of them are natural, such as earthquakes, but others are caused by people. This book will describe some of the disasters that occur when humans upset the natural environment.

RIGHT
The earth provides us with everything we need to live. In order to take care of ourselves, we have to take care of the earth.

RIGHT The purple area in this satellite photograph of the South Pole shows the damage pollution has caused to the ozone layer (see page 6).

Two kinds of environmental disasters are reported in newspapers or on radio and television. There are disasters that result from sudden accidents, which cause a lot of damage, destroy large numbers of wildlife, and sometimes kill or injure many people. The explosion at a chemical factory in Bhopal, India, in 1984 was one example of a terrible accident that led to an environmental disaster (see pages 14–16).

RIGHT This elderly man was one of the 50,000 people who were either injured or killed by gas fumes from the explosion at a chemical factory in Bhopal, India, in 1984.

The other kind of environmental disaster builds up slowly and threatens more people and wildlife than sudden accidents do.

For example, chemicals called chlorofluorocarbons (CFCs) have been used for more than fifty years in the manufacture of refrigerators, aerosol cans, cleaning fluids, and plastic containers. The CFCs in the air drift up into the atmosphere over several years. There, they damage the ozone layer, which protects living things on earth against harmful rays from the sun. The damage to the ozone layer was discovered in the early 1980s and, since then, the nonessential use of CFCs has been outlawed in the U.S. Even so, it will take another fifty years before the ozone layer returns to normal.

DISASTERS ARE WARNINGS

The disasters we read about in newspapers or see on television are warnings to us that we are damaging the environment and should change our ways. If we do not, then we are more likely to suffer from the effects of a poor environment.

In June 1992, many world leaders attended the Earth Summit held in Rio de Janeiro, Brazil. At this meeting the leaders agreed to find ways to protect the environment from further damage.

All of us should make sure that our actions cause as little damage to the environment as possible. We will then be helping to protect the earth from environmental disasters in the future.

ABOVE Senator Al Gore (before he became Vice President of the United States) speaking at the Earth Summit in June 1992. Politicians and environmental groups from around the world met to discuss ways to protect the environment.

NUCLEAR DANGER

ABOVE Large, bustling cities, such as Chicago, Illinois, need enormous amounts of electricity for lighting and heating.

Modern society needs more and more energy every year. We use energy in the form of electricity to heat and light buildings and to work the machinery in factories and offices. Most people living in wealthy countries, such as Canada, the United States, Japan, Britain, and Germany, own various consumer goods, such as cars, television sets, and stoves. Many of these goods use electricity and are made in factories that also use large amounts of electricity.

Most of the electricity we use comes from power plants, some of which are powered by the burning of fuels such as coal, oil, or gas. These fuels are called fossil fuels, and they come from the remains of animals and plants that were deposited in the earth millions of years ago.

Eventually, there will not be enough deposits of fossil fuels left to meet our energy needs, so new sources of energy will have to be developed.

7

THE NUCLEAR AGE

During the early 1940s, scientists learned how to split atoms and collect the energy that held the center, or nucleus, of the atom together. This new source of energy was called atomic, or nuclear, energy.

In 1955, the former U.S.S.R. opened the first nuclear power plant to produce electricity. At the time, newspapers reported that nuclear power would provide us with enough energy for thousands of years. Many countries, including the United States, Britain, and France, built nuclear power plants between the 1950s and 1980s.

Today, many people have a different opinion about the use of nuclear energy. One of the main concerns is safety. When an atom is split to release its energy, radiation is also released. If radioactive material escapes into the atmosphere in large amounts it can

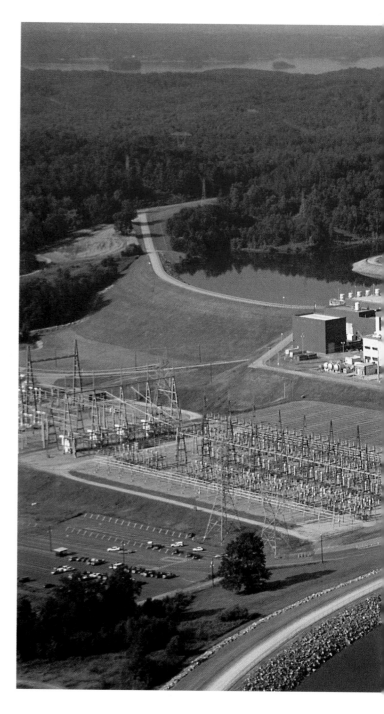

THE NUCLEAR AGE
In 1990
- 421 nuclear power plants were operating.
- 144 nuclear power plants were planned or being built.
- 32 countries had nuclear power plants.
- 70 percent of France's electricity came from nuclear power.
- 33 percent of all nuclear power in the world was generated in the United States.

kill people, wildlife, and plants soon after contact. In smaller doses it can cause diseases, such as cancer.

Nuclear power plants are designed to ensure that, if an accident occurs, complicated emergency systems come into operation and the power plants are shut

ABOVE Nuclear power plants are often built in remote areas. But, if an accident occurs, radiation can travel many miles and reach heavily populated regions.

down automatically. However, when safety systems are complicated to operate there are more chances that equipment will break down or operators will make mistakes.

On April 25, 1986, a tragic accident at the nuclear power plant near Chernobyl, in Ukraine, was caused by human error. The dangerous radiation that leaked from Chernobyl after the accident affected a wide area, including most of Europe.

MAP AS AT 1986

ICELAND

NORWAY

SWEDEN

FINLAND

DENMARK

EIRE

BRITAIN

POLAND

EAST GERMANY

PRIPYAT

WEST GERMANY

CHERNOBYL

KIEV

FRANCE

PORTUGAL

SPAIN

ITALY

GREECE

KEY

AREA AFFECTED BY RADIATION 28 APRIL 1986

AREA AFFECTED BY RADIATION 30 APRIL 1986

AREA AFFECTED BY RADIATION 3 MAY 1986

(FORMER) USSR

N

900 km

560 miles

THE CHERNOBYL CATASTROPHE

The nuclear reaction that provides the energy to operate a power plant is made in the reactors. The atoms are split in the core (center) of the reactor, and this area is full of radiation. If the core of the reactor overheats, a huge explosion could result, which would release the dangerous radiation. To keep the reactor from overheating, a system of safety valves should operate automatically to release the excess heat.

On April 25, 1986, during an experiment in Chernobyl's Unit 4 reactor, safety warnings seem to have been ignored and the automatic safety systems were overridden.

Unfortunately, one of the safety valves became jammed open during the experiment and allowed the radioactive core of the reactor to overheat. No one in the control center of the power plant noticed that the safety valve had failed.

Eventually the operators realized that the experiment was going wrong and tried to stop it. It was too late. At 1:23 A.M. on April 26, there was a huge explosion, which blew off the reactor's roof. Fires broke out sending up eight tons of radioactive material into the atmosphere.

The radioactive cloud covered a large area around Chernobyl and then began to drift west. The local people had not been given any warnings about the accident or the effects of the radiation. When the authorities understood the seriousness of the accident, they moved 135,000 people out of the area.

The radioactive cloud traveled toward Scandinavia and Europe. The cloud reached Poland, Germany, and Sweden by April 28 and swept across mainland Europe to Britain on May 2-3. As the radioactive material fell to the ground in rain, different countries gave different advice about the dangers of radioactive poisoning. In Germany, officials destroyed cereal and vegetable crops because they were thought to be too dangerous to eat. Meanwhile, a few miles away in France, officials claimed that similar crops were safe to eat. Throughout Europe people were worried about drinking milk and eating meat

OPPOSITE TOP A map showing the area affected by the radiation released after the explosion at Chernobyl

OPPOSITE BOTTOM This photograph shows the damage to the nuclear reactor at Chernobyl after the explosion in 1986.

RIGHT The cleanup of the tangled wreckage of the burned-out reactor was a very dangerous job. Due to the high levels of radiation, workers had to wear protective clothing and could work only for short periods at a time.

WITNESS REPORT

PRIPYAT DESERTED

Dr. Robert Gale worked with the Soviet authorities to treat people who had become ill from the effects of radiation. He visited Pripyat, the actual site of the reactor, ten miles northwest of Chernobyl, two years after the accident.

Now all the trees are gone. Two years ago the trees had turned brown from the radiation. Since then they have had to be destroyed. Pripyat's high-rise buildings are deserted. Whilst I was walking around, beautiful operatic music was playing from loudspeakers, but there was no sign of life. It will never be reinhabited (lived in again).

Source: *Chernobyl – The Final Warning* Dr. R. Gale and T. Hauser (London: Hamish Hamilton, 1988).

because some livestock were eating radioactive grass. Even two years after the accident, sheep from some areas of Britain could not be sold for food because they were radioactive.

No one knows how serious the long-term effects of the Chernobyl disaster will be. More than 250 people have died as a direct result of the accident. Over the next forty years, as many as 100,000 people in the former U.S.S.R. may die from different types of cancer caused directly by the accident at Chernobyl. There is a closed area of about 20 miles around the site of the power plant. Some of the towns and villages in the area will never be lived in again because of the high levels of radiation.

THREE-MILE ISLAND

Over the past forty years there have been a number of accidents in nuclear power plants. Seven years before Chernobyl, an accident at Three-Mile Island in Pennsylvania gave clear warning of what could happen if a nuclear reactor were damaged.

On March 28, 1979, a water pump failed in the Unit 2 reactor and the power plant shut down automatically. Unfortunately, the

reactor itself continued working at full power and overheated, which led to the core's overheating.

When news of the accident was reported, 150,000 people fled from the area. Although it cannot be proved that people have died or become ill as a direct result of the Three-Mile Island accident, it showed how easily a disaster could happen. It cost $1 billion and took over ten years to make the reactor safe.

THE FUTURE OF NUCLEAR ENERGY

Using modern technology, nuclear power plants could be made safer. Many scientists support nuclear power because they believe it produces the electricity we need, using a fuel that will last for centuries. Others say that nuclear power is expensive, nuclear waste products are dangerous, and the damage that can be caused by an accident is too terrible to risk.

LEFT *People still live in the residential area close to the Three-Mile Island nuclear power plant.*

CHEMICAL HAZARDS

There are about 70,000 chemicals in use on farms and in factories, offices, homes, and parks – in fact, chemicals are used almost everywhere and for many purposes. At least 35,000 of these chemicals are classed as harmful to human health. For example, many chemicals used at home, such as cleaning liquids or weedkillers, are poisonous if they are swallowed. They should be kept well away from young children.

Some chemicals that are used in industry are so toxic (poisonous) that people working with them have to follow very strict safety rules and wear strong gloves, protective clothing, goggles, and masks when handling them.

CHEMICAL HAZARDS – DANGER TERMS
- "Toxic" describes the chemicals and substances that may cause death or serious injury to humans and animals.
- "Hazardous" is a wider term that describes all chemicals or chemical wastes that are dangerous to people or the environment.

  Most toxic and hazardous chemicals or waste come from industry, especially from factories that make plastics, soaps, detergents, fertilizers, and paints.

Any factory that makes or uses toxic or hazardous chemicals has to be very careful. If there were an accident, such as a fire, the chemicals could get into the environment and cause a lot of damage.

THE BHOPAL CHEMICAL DISASTER
On December 3, 1984, near Bhopal, India, there was an explosion at a chemical factory that made pesticides (chemicals that kill insects). The disaster shocked the world and it is one of the world's worst industrial chemical accidents.

Most of the 750,000 people living in Bhopal were asleep when the accident occurred at 12:30 A.M. About 45 tons of the toxic gas methyl isocyanate spread like a fog over the city and hovered close to the ground. The chemical caused a burning sensation to the eyes and made it difficult to breathe. In the worst-affected areas of the city, hundreds of people died in their sleep – choked to death by the effects of the chemical.

The accident killed at least 2,352 people, but the final total may turn out to be as many as 10,000 people. More than 50,000 people were seriously injured and many of those will suffer from the damage to their lungs or eyesight for the rest of their lives.

In February 1989, Union Carbide, the U.S. company that owned the factory, agreed to pay $470 million to the people who suffered in Bhopal.

ABOVE *Chemicals are used on farms to control the pests and diseases that can damage crops.*

RIGHT *Reports of the terrible accident at the Union Carbide chemical factory near Bhopal, India in 1984 shocked the world.*

Daily Mail
WEDNESDAY, DECEMBER 5, 1984
20p

MONEY MAIL TODAY

The perils behind modern technology...

DEATH CLOUD'S 1,000 VICTIMS

Daily Mail Foreign Service

INDIA has mourned its thousands before, the victims of countless natural disasters. But this one is man-made.

And the 1,000 bodies that littered the shanty towns on the edge of Bhopal died in choking, chemical agony.

They lie now in ragged lines in the grounds of the local hospital which has been swamped by the size of the tragedy—the world's biggest chemical disaster.

Across the afternoon air comes the hacking, choking cough of the lucky ones. Most of them should recover eventually from the effects of the poison gas cloud which engulfed 100,000 people in their makeshift homes.

Others are not so lucky. It is estimated that a total of 20,000 have been affected. Many have lost their sight ; many mothers may not be able to have any more children. The air seems full with the sound of wailing, too . . . the wailing of children who have lost their parents and parents who have lost their children.

Harrowing

Now, two days after the poison gas

15

LEFT *The poisonous gas cloud, which was released after an explosion at the chemical factory, killed thousands of people in Bhopal.*

BELOW *These people fled from Bhopal to escape the gas cloud. Many thousands of people will suffer from the effects of the gas for the rest of their lives.*

WITNESS REPORT

BHOPAL – CHOKED BY A CHEMICAL CLOUD

The dangerous chemical cloud produced by the accident caused widespread panic in the city of Bhopal.

Hundreds of thousands of residents were roused from their sleep, coughing and vomiting and wheezing. Their eyes burned and watered; many would soon be at least temporarily blinded…Those able to board a…vehicle of any kind did. But for most of the poor, their feet were the only form of transport available. Many dropped along the way, gasping for breath, choking on their own vomit and, finally, drowning in their own fluids.

Source: *The Bhopal Syndrome* by David Weir
(London: Earthscan Publication Ltd., 1989).

THE SEVESO ACCIDENT – DANGER OF DIOXIN

The fact that accidents in chemical factories can lead to environmental disasters was known before the Bhopal accident.

On July 10, 1976, there was an explosion at the Icmesa chemical factory near Seveso, Italy. The factory manufactured a powerful weedkiller called 2, 4, 5-T. One of the waste chemicals that is formed while making this weedkiller is called dioxin. Dioxin is one of the most poisonous chemicals ever made. Coming into contact with even a small amount of dioxin can cause health problems, such as heart disease, eye problems, damage to unborn babies, and terrible scarring.

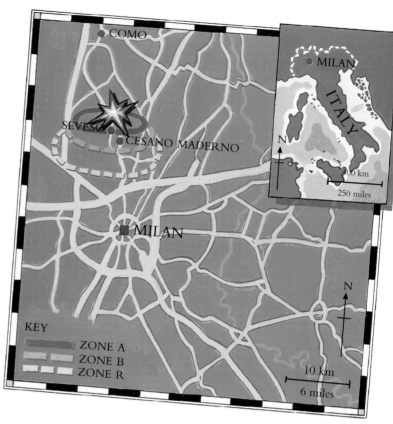

ABOVE A map showing the area affected by the poisonous gas cloud released after an accident at a chemical factory near Seveso, Italy

LEFT The Italian Army stopped people from entering the danger area around Seveso.

The explosion produced a cloud of gas that contained a high level of dioxin. As the cloud traveled over the area around Seveso, 30,000 people were put at risk from the dioxin, which fell from the cloud onto food and crops and into the water supply.

A week after the accident, the authorities told the people not to eat any food grown locally or drink the water. By this time many people had been affected by the dioxin poison.

More than 700 people had to be moved away from the worst-affected area of the town. At least 193 people were seriously injured and more than 500 people were affected in some way by dioxin poisoning. All domestic and livestock animals either died or were destroyed. Even the soil had to be scraped up and buried so that food crops would not be grown in dioxin-poisoned soil.

BELOW Following the accident, all the topsoil from the area surrounding Seveso was removed to keep the dioxin from poisoning any more people.

POISONED WATER

Not all chemical disasters are caused by accidents. In some cases poisonous chemicals are released into the environment when they are purposely poured into rivers or seas as waste.

MINAMATA BAY POISONED

Mercury is a liquid metal that is very toxic. From the 1930s to the 1950s, a local factory used Minamata Bay, in Japan, as a dump for its waste, which contained mercury. The factory owners believed that the mercury would be watered down by the sea and would not cause any harm. However, the mercury was taken in by small sea creatures and these were then eaten by fish. Fishermen caught the poisoned fish, which people then ate – the more seafood they ate, the more poisoned they became.

Since 1953, at least 649 people have died and 1,385 people have been poisoned by the mercury. The company that owned the factory had to pay millions of dollars to the victims or their families.

RIGHT These people were demonstrating at the Earth Summit in June 1992. They want to make sure that incidents like the chemical pollution of Minamata Bay do not happen again.

BELOW RIGHT This child from Minamata Bay, Japan, has been affected by the mercury poisoning.

WITNESS REPORT

MERCURY POISONING AT MINAMATA BAY

Minamata Bay, in Japan, had been polluted by mercury since the 1930s. However, it was only in the early 1950s that scientists and doctors reported the terrible effects that the mercury was having on animals and people in the area.

Terrible things had been happening in the fishing villages to the north and south of the town....The cats here started going mad, dancing around, hissing and yowling, attacking their owners, toppling over, throwing themselves into the sea and drowning. Gulls and crows would stall (stop moving) in midflight and plunge into the water....Then it started happening to the people...their fingers and toes had gone numb or they could no longer see properly or walk straight....Children and adults alike began to die. Source: *The Independent Magazine* (London), May 11, 1991.

SANDOZ – THE RHINE RIVER POISONED

The Rhine River flows through Switzerland, Germany, and The Netherlands, and there are many chemical factories and warehouses along its banks. On November 1, 1986, a fire broke out in a warehouse belonging to the Sandoz chemical company in Basle, Switzerland. The warehouse stored very hazardous chemicals, which were used to make pesticides.

ABOVE Dangerous chemicals leaked into the Rhine River after a fire at the Sandoz warehouse in Switzerland, in 1986.

Basle has so many chemical factories and warehouses that store chemicals that the city has a separate fire brigade with specially-trained firefighters who deal with chemical emergencies.

Unfortunately, the fire at the Sandoz warehouse happened at night when these special firefighters were off duty. The ordinary fire brigade managed to control the fire but did not know how to deal with the dangerous chemicals.

The containers holding the chemicals burst open in the heat and the chemicals mixed with the water from the fire hoses and washed into the river. The chemicals killed almost all the water life in the river, including 500,000 fish, for a distance of nearly 200 miles.

It will take at least ten years for the Rhine to recover from this environmental disaster.

ABOVE RIGHT The chemicals that were washed into the Rhine after the Sandoz accident killed most of the fish and plants in the river for almost 200 miles.

BELOW In this picture you can see the burned remains of the chemical containers.

WASTE NOT, WANT NOT

THE THROW-AWAY SOCIETY

Everyone makes waste. Waste is all the things that we no longer want or need, such as empty bottles and cans, old newspapers, packaging, broken radios, television sets, and other electrical equipment.

In one day, people in the United States throw away 90 million bottles, 46 million cans, and 25,000 television sets. Most of this kind of waste is dumped in massive holes in the ground called landfills. Some of the waste contains hazardous chemicals. For example, old paints may contain lead, which can cause blood poisoning.

DANGERS OF LANDFILLS

Over a period of time, the layers of waste build up and the temperature inside the landfill rises, which helps some waste to rot. This produces methane, a gas that burns easily. Usually, a system of pipes collects the gas so that it can escape into the atmosphere (where it harms the ozone) or can be used as a fuel. If the methane is not collected it can seep through the ground and build up in an enclosed space, such as a building. A spark could cause the gas to explode and start a fire.

Poisonous liquids also form in the waste. If the landfill is not watertight these hazardous liquids can seep into rivers and reservoirs that supply drinking water.

ABOVE *Most of the waste from households, and some waste from industry, ends up in landfills.*

LIVING ON A WASTE DUMP

Many countries have old landfills that no one knows about until they start to cause problems. This report from a British newspaper describes the worrying events that happened to a group of people living in Portsmouth, a town on the south coast of England.

Families on a Portsmouth housing estate (a development) were sunning themselves this summer (1991) when a group of men in white overalls and breathing masks suddenly arrived and started digging holes.

"It was a bit odd," recalls Theresa Foster, mother of three. "We were sitting around and these men, also in protective gloves, mumbled through their masks that it was important for us not to worry."

The houses had been built on an old waste tip (dump) that had belonged to the navy. When some unused land nearby was being sold, a survey revealed dangerous chemicals in the soil. The land where the houses were built was also found to be contaminated (poisoned). The workmen's report called for urgent action.

"We were having our tea when council officers arrived to tell us we should leave immediately."

In total, 216 people were removed from their homes.

Source: *The Independent* (London), November 2, 1991.

ABOVE *This is the housing development in Portsmouth, England that had to be evacuated in 1991.*

DISASTER AT LOVE CANAL

The most famous disaster concerning an old landfill site was at Love Canal, in New York State. During the 1940s and 1950s a local factory buried poisonous waste in metal drums. The site was then sold and a housing development was built on the old landfill.

In 1978, dioxin from the buried waste was found in nearby water supplies and in the soil around people's homes. The chemicals inside the drums had leaked underground and had poisoned the whole area.

The United States government declared Love Canal a disaster area. People from

239 homes were moved away immediately; later, another 710 families had to leave their homes.

No one knows if any of the people living in Love Canal got sick as a result of this disaster, but the government has tried to make sure that it never happens again. In 1980, the Environmental Protection Agency (EPA) began a search for all the old landfill sites that would need to be cleaned. So many dangerous sites were found that it will take fifty years and cost many millions of dollars to clean all the dumps.

ABOVE TOP The housing development at Love Canal was built on top of a landfill. The people who lived there had to move because dangerous chemicals began to leak from containers under the ground.
ABOVE A landfill site being tested for poisonous chemicals

THE WASTE TRADE

Most people do not like the idea of having toxic waste dumped near where they live or work. Companies have to find other ways to get rid of the dangerous waste produced by industry.

Some of this poisonous waste is dumped into the sea, and this can damage the marine life very badly. The poisons are taken in by small creatures that are then eaten by bigger fish. These poisoned fish are eaten by larger creatures, such as whales and seals, and these are poisoned and get sick. In 1988 a mystery disease killed more than 14,000 seals in the North Sea. It was believed that toxic chemicals, called polychlorinated biphenyls (PCBs), had washed into the sea and were damaging the seals' ability to fight the disease. PCBs are found in industrial waste. This waste sometimes gets into rivers and then into the sea.

RIGHT Many people believe that dumping waste at sea damages marine wildlife.

WITNESS REPORT

OUR SEAS – THE SECRET WASTE DUMPS

Sometimes waste disappears without a record of where it has been dumped. In 1989, *Green Magazine* reported that some dangerous waste was being "lost" at sea.

"It all gets done in secrecy," said Captain Hubert Wardleman, (from)...the International Maritime Organization.

"When I was at sea it was commonplace that there would arrive a few hundred drums of waste in Antwerp (in Belgium) on a barge. The master (captain) would be asked to take it and when he was on the high sea, to throw it overboard. I always said no."

Source: *Green Magazine* (London), November 1989.

KARIN B – THE UNWANTED CARGO

Companies in industrialized countries, such as the United States and Japan, will pay a lot of money to other countries to take their dangerous waste. So, more and more toxic or hazardous waste is being transported by sea.

Sometimes, shipping companies have found it difficult to find a country that will take the waste. Between July and August 1988, the cargo ship *Karin B* sailed from country to country trying to unload its cargo of poisonous waste, which had been picked up from Nigeria, in Africa. The ship was refused entry to Italy, Germany, Spain, and Britain. Eventually Italy was forced to accept the cargo and dispose of it safely, because the waste had originally been sent to Nigeria by an Italian company.

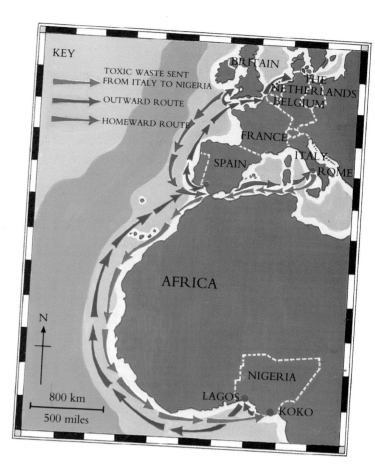

ABOVE *The cargo of dangerous chemicals was sent from Italy and stored near the town of Koko, Nigeria. After local people got sick, the* Karin B *was sent to pick up the cargo. The ship was refused entry to Spain, France, Belgium, The Netherlands, Germany, and Britain before being forced to return to Italy.*

LEFT *The* Karin B*'s cargo of poisonous waste was picked up from Nigeria, Africa, where it had been stored illegally and had caused local people to get sick.*

OIL ON THE WATERS

Oil is one of the most important products in use in the world today. It is used in power plants to make electricity and in motor vehicles. Oil is also a raw material, which is used to make some chemicals and plastics.

TRANSPORTING OIL

Huge amounts of oil are shipped around the world every day in giant ships called "supertankers." Some of these ships can carry up to 275,000 tons of oil. Fortunately, there are few accidents involving these enormous tankers. However, when an accident does occur, and a large amount of oil escapes into the sea, the environment can be badly damaged.

BELOW The giant oil tanker, Torrey Canyon, *ran aground in March 1967. More than 130,000 tons of oil poured into the seas around Cornwall, England.*

THE DANGER OF SUPERTANKERS

One of the first supertanker accidents occurred in March 1967 when the *Torrey Canyon*, carrying 132,000 tons of oil, crashed on rocks off the south coast of England. The rocks ripped a 650-foot gash along her hull (the outside shell), and the cargo of oil poured into the sea. Over the next ten days the oil spill covered over 700 square miles of ocean and began to wash up on the shores of Britain and France. An attempt was made to bomb the stricken tanker to set fire to the remaining cargo of oil, but this did not work. Eventually, the ship broke up in the water.

Thousands of people helped in the cleanup operations along the coasts, but the damage caused to the environment and wildlife was terrible – 100,000 seabirds were covered with oil and many other marine animals were killed or badly affected by the oil.

EXXON VALDEZ – A WILDERNESS DAMAGED

The oil spill from the supertanker *Exxon Valdez*, in 1989, shocked the world. It is the worst oil spill to occur in U.S. waters and took place in Prince William Sound, one of Alaska's most important wildlife and fishing areas.

On March 24, 1989, the supertanker ran aground on rocks and the hull split open.

BELOW TOP More than 38,500 tons of oil spilled from the Exxon Valdez *into the waters of Prince William Sound, Alaska.*

BELOW BOTTOM Hundreds of people worked to clean the oil from the beaches and coastline of Alaska.

More than 38,500 tons of oil escaped. The oil companies in charge of emergency cleanup operations were slow to react to the disaster and failed to keep the oil from spreading. The spill reached the tip of the Alaska Peninsula, 560 miles away. A cleanup operation, costing $843 million, took place, but at least 980 sea otters, 146 bald eagles, and 33,100 other birds died. Scientists working for the U.S. government reported that the total number of animals lost is probably ten times greater, but the bodies had been washed ashore in remote areas or had sunk.

WITNESS REPORT

"MAKE SURE IT DOESN'T HAPPEN AGAIN"

This is a comment from Dan Lawn, who helped to organize the cleanup operation in Prince William Sound, Alaska, after the *Exxon Valdez* oil spill.

This spill has really changed me and a lot of us. I've had to deal with emotions I've never experienced before. When you see birds pulling feathers out until they make holes in their necks and oiled otters that show no resistance (struggle) *when you pick them up, it brings it home to you what an oil spill really means. We need to do whatever is necessary to make sure it doesn't happen again.*

Source: *New Scientist* (London), August 12, 1989.

ABOVE *Fortunately, when the* Braer *oil tanker ran aground on the coast of the Shetland Islands, strong winds and large waves broke up most of the oil.*

LEFT *This rescued sea otter was covered with oil and might have died if it had not been found.*

THE *BRAER* OIL SPILL

Even after the *Torrey Canyon* and *Exxon Valdez* disasters, the seas are still under threat from oil spills.

On January 5, 1993, the *Braer* oil tanker crashed on the coast of the Shetland Islands, in the North Sea.

The *Braer* had been carrying 92,000 tons of oil from Norway to Canada when it lost power during a very bad storm. The crew was taken off the ship before the storm forced the tanker onto the rocks. The tanker's hull broke in two and more than 44,000 tons of oil began to pour into the sea. Within a week of the accident, the oil spill had killed more than 700 birds and had affected large numbers of seals and sea otters. The oil also affected livestock and farmland on the island, because sea spray and rain left a covering of oil over grass, crops, and animals.

The *Braer* finally broke up on January 13, and the remaining 48,900 tons of oil spilled into the sea.

A cleanup operation was prevented by terrible storms. Fortunately, the heavy seas and strong winds helped to break up the oil spill very quickly.

Unfortunately, such a terrible environmental disaster is likely to have many long-term effects on the Shetland Islands, especially on the health of the wildlife and fish stocks in the area.

AT WAR WITH THE ENVIRONMENT

When people fight wars, they want to win at any cost – even if it means destroying the environment. The environment can be damaged by warfare in many ways: by bombs, poisonous gases, or oil pollution that results from the destruction of storage tanks or ships. Often there is no way of trying to clean up the damage until the war is over, which can be too late.

VIETNAM'S LOST FORESTS

In the Vietnam War (1964-75), U.S. forces joined the South Vietnamese army against the North Vietnamese and the Vietcong armies.

Much of Vietnam was thick tropical rain forest. During the war, soldiers could move around in the forests without being seen from the air. In order to see the positions of enemy troops, the U.S. forces used a powerful herbicide (a chemical that kills plants or trees) called "Agent Orange." Thousands of bombs containing Agent Orange were dropped on the rain forests to clear large areas. Bulldozers were used to remove the trees and soil so that the plants would not grow again. During the war,

LEFT Millions of gallons of the herbicide Agent Orange were sprayed on the rain forests by U.S. aircraft during the Vietnam War.

OPPOSITE BELOW The areas of rain forest that were most severely damaged by Agent Orange were along the border between South Vietnam and Cambodia.

WITNESS REPORT

A TROPICAL RAIN FOREST TURNED INTO A "WHITE ZONE"

The combination of bombs... bulldozers, and herbicides had turned our tropical forest into a "white zone." More than 2 million hectares of forest and land were destroyed during the... raids that rained 72 million litres of herbicides on southern Vietnam. Source: *BBC Wildlife Magazine* (Bristol, England), December 1991.

ABOVE Chemicals such as Agent Orange can reduce a thick rain forest to a few bare stumps.

20 percent of Vietnam's rain forests were destroyed along with the birds and animals that lived in them.

Today, the people of Vietnam are trying to make their country green again. For example, all students plant at least one tree a year as part of their studies. Each year, almost 400,000 acres of forest are planted to replace some of the 5 million acres that were destroyed during the war.

THE GULF WAR OIL DAMAGE

Most of the world's oil is produced by countries in the Persian Gulf region. These countries include Iraq, Kuwait, Saudi Arabia, United Arab Emirates, Iran, Qatar, and Oman.

On August 2, 1990, Iraqi troops took Kuwait by force. This action began the Gulf War (1990-91).

After months of talks between the members of the United Nations (UN), an Allied attack, which lasted from January 17 to March 3, 1991, freed Kuwait from the Iraqi troops.

Unfortunately, besides great loss of life, the Gulf War caused two environmental disasters.

The first disaster began on January 25, 1991 when a massive oil spill appeared from one of Kuwait's oil terminals on the Persian Gulf. The oil spill covered 285 miles of the Kuwaiti and Saudi Arabian coasts. The thick oil damaged coral reefs, sandy beaches, headlands, and mangrove (salt water) swamps where large numbers of wildlife lived. More than 30,000 birds died and other marine life was badly affected.

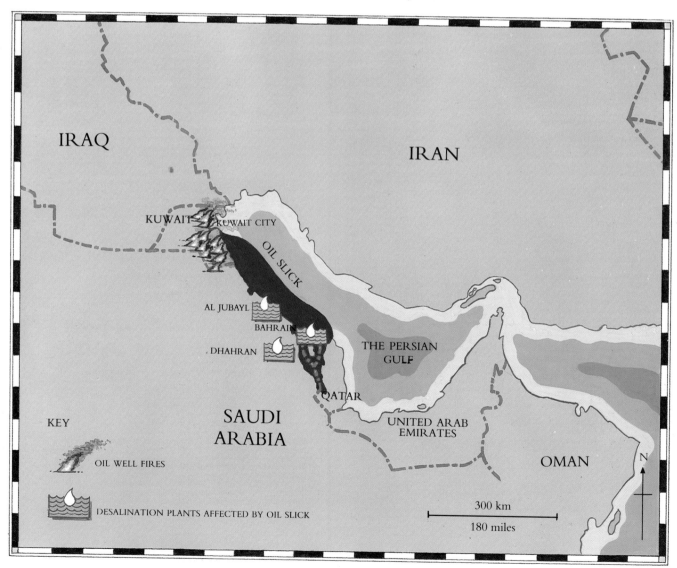

IRAQ

IRAN

KUWAIT
KUWAIT CITY

OIL SLICK

AL JUBAYL

BAHRAIN

THE PERSIAN GULF

DHAHRAN

QATAR

SAUDI ARABIA

UNITED ARAB EMIRATES

OMAN

N

KEY

OIL WELL FIRES

DESALINATION PLANTS AFFECTED BY OIL SLICK

300 km
180 miles

ABOVE *During the Gulf War, an oil spill poured into the Persian Gulf. The Kuwaiti and Saudi Arabian coasts were covered with oil, and coral reefs were badly damaged.*

RIGHT *This soldier is holding up an oil-soaked fish.*

OPPOSITE *This map of the Persian Gulf region shows the fields of oil wells in Kuwait that were set alight and the oil slick that covered 285 miles of Kuwaiti and Saudi Arabian coastline.*

A BLACK CLOUD OVER THE GULF

During the Allied attack on the Iraqi forces, the Iraqi troops began to set fire to 850 of Kuwait's oil wells. The thick dirty smoke from the fires darkened the skies and many people had breathing problems.

All the oil well fires are out now, but the oil is still causing problems. A lot of oil escaped and flooded the land, making large oil lakes that smothered anything living there. Some birds have been poisoned when trying to drink from the lakes, mistaking them for water. It will take years before we know what the long-term effects of the Gulf War will be on the environment.

RIGHT *Oil escaped from the wells that had been set alight and formed huge lakes in the desert.*
OPPOSITE *The smoke was so thick that it shut out the sun.*

WITNESS REPORT

DARK AT NOON IN KUWAIT CITY

Dr. Safein, a doctor working in Kuwait City, describes the effect of the smoke from the oil well fires.

Darkness at noon frightens the patients.... In the hospitals there is no sanctuary (safety) from the oily smoke.... Already the orange trees in the city center have started to wilt; even the birds are dying, falling out of the sky and hopping about in agony until they keel over. Now it is the turn of the humans to suffer.
Source: *The* [London] *Observer*, March 24, 1991.

LEFT *The smoke from the oil-well fires filled the air in and around Kuwait City.*

STRIPPING THE EARTH

Thousands of years ago, humans began to clear land of its natural vegetation, such as trees, bushes, and grasses, to be able to grow crops or raise livestock.

Over the years, the need for more and more food and the invention of more efficient farm machinery has led to the creation of huge stretches of farmland with no permanent natural vegetation.

SOIL EROSION

Natural vegetation is important because it protects the soil from the weather by keeping heavy rain from flowing across the surface or by stopping the wind from blowing the soil away. When soil is exposed to the weather, or when it is used to grow the same crops year after year, it becomes infertile and cannot grow anything at all. In this way, fertile farmland can be turned into desert. That is what happened to a large area of farmland in the Midwest of the United States during the 1930s.

LEFT Large areas of forest are being cut down around the world, especially in Africa and South America. Once the soil is exposed to the hot sun and heavy rain it gets washed away quickly.

RIGHT An aerial view of a dust storm forming in Oklahoma

THE GREAT DUST BOWL DISASTER

During the 1920s, farmers in the south-central United States plowed up great areas of grassland and planted cereal crops, such as wheat. To earn more money from their land, the farmers grew crops all the time instead of "resting" the land to allow the soil to recover. They also let livestock overgraze. The land became exhausted and the crops failed.

Between 1930 and 1931 there were two years of drought. The overworked soil became dry and fine. In 1934, a gale (very strong wind) swept across the country, and it picked up more than 385,000 tons of dust from the drought-stricken Midwest. The dust storm traveled toward the east coast and blotted out the sun, plunging cities such as New York and Washington, DC into darkness during the daytime. It was clear that the United States had suffered a major environmental disaster.

WITNESS REPORT

THE GREAT DUST BOWL

An American newspaper reporter named Albert Law wrote about the Dust Bowl disaster in the early 1930s.

Not a blade of wheat in Cimarron County, Oklahoma; cattle dying there on the range; a few bushels of wheat in the Perryton area against an average yield (crop) of 4-6 million bushels...90 percent of the poultry dead because of sandstorms...hogs (pigs) in such...shape that buyers will not have them.

Source: *Battle for the Planet* by André Singer (London: Pan Books/Channel 4).

ABOVE This photograph shows a dust storm in South Dakota – one of the states that formed the Great Dust Bowl in the 1930s.

FAMINE IN ETHIOPIA & SOMALIA

In recent years, we have read reports in newspapers and seen pictures on television of the millions of people dying of hunger in some countries in Africa – especially Ethiopia and Somalia. These countries have suffered from terrible famines because the farmland could not grow crops as a result of soil erosion and drought. Trees used to cover 30 percent of the land in Ethiopia, but now only 3 percent of the land has any trees. The trees have been cut down for firewood and to clear land to raise cattle. The soil became damaged because it was exposed to the hot sun and the cattle overgrazed the land.

Between 1983 and 1985 there was a drought in Ethiopia, which caused the failure of crops and the death of livestock in certain areas. As a result of this environmental disaster, 1 million people died of starvation.

When reports of the disaster were read in newspapers and seen on television many people wanted to help the suffering people in Ethiopia. Large amounts of money were given to help international organizations, such as Save the Children, to provide food and medicine to the Ethiopian people. Many thousands of lives were saved because of this aid.

The work to help the people of Ethiopia is still going on today. Many of the organizations have worked with the Ethiopian government to set up training programs. People are being taught farming methods that will help the soil to recover, reducing the risk of another famine in the future.

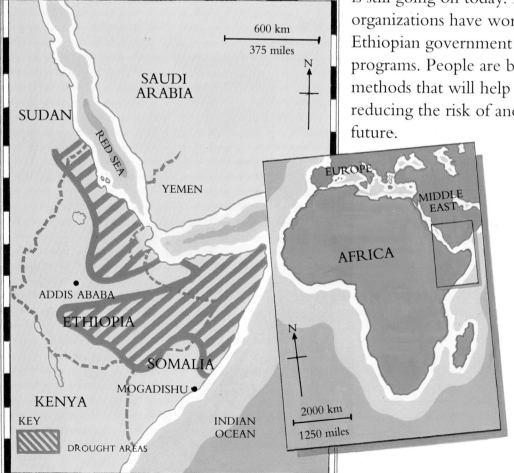

RIGHT *In the mid-1980s, reports and pictures of the people suffering from famine and drought in Ethiopia were shown on television and printed in newspapers all over the world.*

LEFT *This map of East Africa shows the drought-stricken areas in Sudan, Ethiopia, and Somalia.*

LEFT *The recent famine in Somalia has affected millions of people. International aid organizations have set up food stations and have helped many thousands of people.*

BELOW *Sacks of food being unloaded at the port of Mogadishu, Somalia. The food will be transported across country to the food stations.*

SOMALIA IN DANGER

Somalia, one of Ethiopia's neighbors, has also suffered from a recent famine. In 1992, it was reported that 300,000 people had died of starvation and 2 million more were at risk.

Again, when the disaster in Somalia was reported in newspapers and on television, people gave money to organizations to send aid. Unfortunately, even though thousands of tons of aid were delivered to Somalia, relief workers were not able to get it through to the neediest areas.

Somalia was involved in a civil war (when the people of a country fight against each other). The fighting made it dangerous for the relief workers to travel in the country, so many people continued to die of hunger.

On December 7, 1992, the U.S. government sent troops into Somalia to help guard and distribute the aid around the country. The operation was called "Restore Hope," but it will be some time before we know if it has helped the people of Somalia.

DANGER IN THE AIR

Air pollution can damage the health of people and wildlife. Factories and motor vehicles are the main cause of air pollution because they burn fuel. When fuels such as coal, oil, or gasoline are burned, they produce smoke and poisonous fumes, which mix with the air that we breathe. Factories also create soot, dust, and dirt that contain harmful substances, such as lead, which can be poisonous.

LEFT The air in cities can become so polluted by smoke and car fumes that some people protect their lungs by wearing masks.

ABOVE Cubatao, in Brazil, is one of the most polluted cities in the world.

The most common effects of air pollution are breathing problems and skin disorders. The people and wildlife that live in cities and industrialized areas are most at risk from these effects. Sometimes air pollution can even kill.

THE AIR THAT WE BREATHE

Every winter, until 1962, there were days in Britain when many cities were covered by foul-smelling smog – a mixture of fog with smoke and chemical fumes produced by fires in houses and factories.

The smog that covered London between December 5 and 9, 1952 was much worse than normal. People had difficulty breathing the dirty air and the numbers of people dying in the capital rose from 250 to 1,000 a day. This disaster encouraged the British Government to produce the 1956 Clean Air Act that forced people in the worst-affected areas to burn smokeless fuels. Most cities and other badly affected areas of Britain were made "smokeless zones." It took six years for the new laws to reduce air pollution levels, but London has not suffered from smog since 1962.

Today, other countries also have strict laws and rules about air pollution levels. Unfortunately, smog is still a problem for some major cities, such as Los Angeles, California and Mexico City, Mexico.

KRAKÓW, POLAND – POLLUTION HOVERS OVERHEAD

Kraków is one of the most industrialized areas of Poland. Unfortunately, it is also one of the most polluted cities in the world. There are two major reasons for the dangerous levels of pollution in the city. One problem is the fact that most of the factories in Kraków use out-of-date machinery, which creates a lot of smoke and pollution. Also, the city lies in a valley and the pollution is trapped by the sides of the valley and hovers over the city – in winter, the city is often covered by smog.

Over 60 percent of the people living in Kraków suffer ill health as a direct result of the pollution. The Nova Huta steelworks, in Kraków, is one of the unhealthiest places to

work in the world. Doctors' records have shown that 8 percent of the people working at the factory will die from illnesses caused by the smoke, dirt, and other pollution, and 80 percent of the work force will retire because of serious illness caused by the pollution.

LEFT Many countries in Eastern Europe have some of the world's dirtiest factories. The people, wildlife, and vegetation suffer from the dense air pollution.

WARMER AIR ACTS LIKE A LID AND PREVENTS POLLUTION FROM RISING HIGHER

POLLUTION STAYS IN VALLEY AND HOVERS OVER THE CITY

VALLEY SIDES

COOL AIR COLLECTS IN THE VALLEY

VALLEY SIDES

RIVER VISTULA

The problem of Kraków's air pollution cannot be solved quickly. It will cost a lot of money and take many years to modernize all the factories in the city. Unfortunately, Poland is not a rich country, so the people of Kraków will have to suffer with the pollution for the forseeable future.

A WARNING TO US ALL

Most people want to make their lives more comfortable and enjoyable. Many people have benefited from the use of modern technology in agriculture and industry, such as new weedkillers and machinery. But sometimes we are greedy – we want all the benefits of an improved life-style without paying the costs of protecting the environment from damage. The environmental disasters described in this book should be a warning to us all. To look after ourselves, we must look after the earth.

GLOSSARY

Atmosphere The air that surrounds the earth.

Atoms Tiny particles, too small to be seen, of which all things are made.

Cancer A disease that affects body cells so that they grow too quickly.

Cargo The load carried by a ship or an airplane.

Drought Lack of rain and water.

Environmental Protection Agency (EPA) A department of the U.S. Government that looks into the causes and extent of damage to the environment.

Famine Lack of food over a wide area.

Industry The manufacturing of goods, usually in factories.

Manufacture To make finished goods out of raw materials.

Ozone layer The layer of gases in the earth's atmosphere that protects the earth from harmful ultraviolet light from the sun.

Radiation The sending and spreading out of energy. We are surrounded by harmless background radiation from our natural environment – from rocks, air, and water – but high doses of radiation produced by nuclear energy are very dangerous to living things.

Radioactive Giving off nuclear radiation.

Raw materials Things in nature that can be made into products. For example, trees give us wood to build houses, and oil can be made into plastic.

Reactors The areas in nuclear power plants where atoms are split and their energy changed into heat.

United Nations An organization to which most countries belong, which was formed to work toward world peace and protect the rights of all the countries of the world.

Vegetation All plants, such as grasses, bushes, and trees.

USEFUL ADDRESSES

Environmental Defense Fund
1616 P Street NW Suite 150
Washington, DC 20036

Environmental Law Institute
1616 P Street NW, Suite 200
Washington, DC 20036

Environmental Protection Agency
401 M Street SW
Washington, DC 20460

Friends of the Earth
218 D Street SE
Washington, DC 20003

Greenpeace
1436 U Street NW
Washington, DC 20009

The Nature Conservancy
1815 Lynn Street
Arlington, VA 22209

FURTHER READING

Baines, John. *Exploring Humans and the Environment*. Austin: Raintree Steck-Vaughn, 1992.

Bellamy, David. *How Green Are You?* New York: Crown Books for Young Readers, 1991.

Doney, Meryl. *The Green Activity Book*. Batavia, Ill: Lion USA, 1991.

Hare, Tony. *Domestic Waste*. Save Our Earth. New York: Gloucester Press, 1992.

Harris, Colin. *Protecting the Planet*. Young Geographer. New York: Thomson Learning, 1993.

Koral, April. *Our Global Greenhouse*. First Books. New York: Franklin Watts, 1989.

Middleton, Nick. *Atlas of Environmental Issues*. New York: Facts On File, 1989.

Seidenberg, Steven. *Ecology and Conservation*. Milwaukee: Gareth Stevens, 1990.

United States Committee for the United Nations Environment Program
2013 Q Street NW
Washington, DC 20009

World Wildlife Fund
1250 24th Street
Washington, DC 20037

PICTURE ACKNOWLEDGMENTS

Camera Press 20 (bottom) (S. Kuwabara), 30-31 (M. Gilfeather), 39; Ecoscene 24; The Environmental Picture Library 6 (H. Girardet); Explorer cover (background) (C. Boisvieux), 5 (top) (NASA), 36 (bottom) (P. Wysocki); John Frost Historical Newspaper Service 15; Greenpeace Media Ltd 21 (Vennemann), 23 (Brook), 30 (both) (Merjeburgh), 43 (Top) (Morgan); Impact Photos Ltd cover (inset), 11 (V. Ivleva), 26 (J. Swift), 35 (bottom) (J. Staquet /Cedri), 37 (M. Ansar), 42 (left) (J. Sterneklar), 43 (left) (S. Shepheard), 44-5 (G. Lewis); NHPA 4-5 (ANT), 7 (G. Gainsburgh); Photri 8-9 (B.Barley), 32-3, 35 (top); Popperfoto Ltd 14-15, 28, 36 (top) (AFP), 38-9; Rex Features Ltd 5 (bottom) (T. Haley),12-13 (T. Haley), 16 (top) (M. Sinh), 17-18 (A. Pesteguy), 18 (inset) (A. Pesteguy), 22 (bottom) (ASL), 27 (Today), 29 (both) (J. Schult), 38 (left) (Nicolas), 40 (T. McGrath), 42 (right) (Merlet); Frank Spooner Pictures 25 (top); Still Pictures Ltd 20 (top) (M. Edwards); Topham Picture Library 10, 16 (bottom), 22 (top), 33 (bottom),40-41; ZEFA 19 (G. Palmer), 25 (both) (G. Palmer).

All illustrations by Tony Jackson.

INDEX

Numbers in **bold** indicate photographs.

Africa   27, 40-42

Bhopal chemical disaster, India
   5, **5**, 14-16, **14-16**
Braer oil spill, Shetland Islands
   30-31, 31
Britain   7, 8, 11, 12, 24, 27,
   28-29, 43
   Clean Air Act, Britain (1956)   44

Canada   **6**, 7, 31
chemical disasters
   Bhopal, India   5, **5**, 14-16, **14-16**
   Minamata Bay, Japan   19-20, **20**
   Sandoz, Switzerland   21-22,
   21, 22
   Seveso, Italy   17-18, **17, 18**
Chernobyl catastrophe, Ukraine
   (former U.S.S.R.)   9, 10-12,
   10, 11
   radioactive cloud   11

dioxin poisoning   17-18, 24-25
   Love Canal, NY   24-25, **25**
   Seveso, Italy   17-18, **17, 18**
Dust Bowl, U.S.   38-39, **38, 39**

Earth Summit   6, **6**
electricity   7-9
   fossil fuels   7
   nuclear energy   8-9
Environmental Protection Agency
   (U.S. Government)   25
Ethiopia   40-41, **40, 41**
Exxon Valdez oil spill, Alaska
   29-30, **29, 30**

famine   40-42
France   8, 11, 29

Germany   7, 11, 21, 27

Italy   17-18, 27

Japan   7, 19-20, 27

Karin B - unwanted cargo   27, **27**
Kuwait   34-36

Love Canal, NY   24-25, **25**

Minamata Bay mercury
   poisoning, Japan   19-20, **20**

Netherlands, The   21
Nigeria   27
North Sea
   Braer oil spill   **30-31**, 31
   seal virus   26, **26**
Norway   30
nuclear dangers   7-13
   atoms   8
   Chernobyl, Ukraine (former
      U.S.S.R.)   9, 10-12, **10, 11**
   radiation   8
   reactors   10

oil spills
   Braer, Shetland Islands   **30-31**, 31
   Exxon Valdez, Alaska   29-30,
      29, 30
   Torrey Canyon, England   28-29,
      28
ozone layer   **5**, 6
   chlorofluorocarbons (CFCs)   6
   methane   23

Persian Gulf   34-37
pesticides   21
Poland   11, 44-45
   Kraków   44-45
pollution
   air   43-45
   land   23-25
   rivers and seas   19-22, 26-27,
      28-31

radiation   8, 11-12
   Chernobyl, Ukraine (former
      U.S.S.R.)   9, 10-12, **10, 11**
   Three-Mile Island, PA   12-13,
      12-13
rain forests
   land clearing 38
   Vietnam War, effect of 32-33,
      32-33
Rhine River poisoned   21-22, **22**

Sandoz chemical leak, Switzerland
   21-22, **21, 22**
Saudi Arabia   34
Seveso dioxin disaster, Italy
   17-18, **17, 18**
smog   43-45
soil erosion   38-40
Somalia   42, **42**
Spain   27
Switzerland   21

Three-Mile Island radiation leak,
   U.S.   12-13, **12-13**
Torrey Canyon oil spill   28-29, **28**

United Nations (UN)   34
United States   7, 8, 12-13, 23,
   24-25, 27, 29-30, 32-33, 38-39,
   42, 44
   U.S.S.R. (former)   8, 9, 10-12,
      10, 11

Vietnam War (1964-75)
   Agent Orange, use of   32-33,
      32, 33

Waste pollution
   Karin B   27, **27**
   landfills   23, **23**
   Love Canal, NY   24-25, **25**
   Minamata Bay, Japan   19-20, **20**